D1446825

Compassion

Arloa Sutter

wesleyan
publishing
house

Indianapolis, Indiana

Contents

Introduction: Compassion for the Poor

In the wake of growing economic disparity and social unrest, a new generation of Christians is awakening to God's call to care for the poor.

For years, many Christians in the United States have lived in isolated bubbles of prosperity untouched by the suffering of our less fortunate brothers and sisters. Concerns about the poor have seemed distant, and we have rarely been forced to think about them.

However, a spiraling economy, changing demographics, and global connectedness are waking us from our slumber. When we see friends and family members being crushed under the weight of unemployment, it moves us to discover what the Bible teaches about caring for those in need. As communities grow in social and economic diversity, church leaders often struggle to know how to effectively demonstrate compassion to the hurting in their communities.

At some level, most of us feel that we should be doing something to care for the poor, but we are not sure what. We know, for example, that some forms of charity can do more harm than good to the people we are trying to help. We may have tried to help struggling friends or acquaintances to get on their feet only to find the issues they face so complicated that we wonder whether there is anything to be done that would genuinely help.

Some believe people are poor only because they are lazy and that if people would just make better choices, they could surely escape the jaws of poverty. We have heard of athletes, politicians, and other celebrities who have escaped the poverty of their past and are living the good life. Why can't others seem to break loose from the crush of poverty?

Some are swayed by theological arguments that suggest helping the poor is a hopeless task, irrelevant in the light of eternity, and peripheral to the gospel. Some suspect that caring about the poor is somehow tied to a social gospel or a left-wing socialist agenda.

While there are many reasons Christians might hold back from involving themselves with the poor, the Bible is clear that the gospel is good news for the poor as well as for us. As we will see in this study, Scripture teaches that care for the poor is central to what it means to follow Christ and that our lives will be positively transformed by associating with the poor.

This study guide is a tool for Christians, churches, and small groups who are seeking a fuller understanding of what it means to follow Jesus, especially in light of his mission to "preach good news to the poor" (Luke 4:18). The lessons are designed to facilitate thought and discussion about passages of Scripture that will introduce you to a deeper understanding of God's heart for the poor and how the church can find and serve "the least of these" (Matt. 25:40). It will equip you and your small group with principles from Scripture that will move you to care for the poor in your own backyard and across the world in more meaningful and effective ways.

Are you ready to have your life transformed by the Word of God?

How to Use This Study Guide

This study guide is a companion study for my book, *The Invisible: What the Church Can Do to Find and Serve the Least of These*. If you have not already read *The Invisible*, you may want to purchase and read it before you embark on this study. You will find it a helpful backdrop to read what I learned from my personal journey into a deeper understanding of God's heart for the poor.

This study is designed in a workbook format for both individual study and group discussion. Each of the four group discussions are sub-divided into five studies for you to do on your own. If you commit to read the daily Scripture passages throughout the week and reflect on the questions which are provided at the end of each section, you will be prepared for the group discussion. You will need to devote about half an hour five times during the week for your personal study time. The larger group weekly discussion is designed to take about an hour.

At the beginning of each lesson, you will read a brief narrative to introduce the study. Then you will read Scripture passages and answer the questions provided. You may want to read the Scriptures several times in order to reflect upon their meaning. Write out your answers to the questions that follow in a journal or notebook. This will help you express your thoughts clearly. This will also allow you to add any comments or questions that may develop when you meet with your small group.

Each day, one of the verses will be highlighted for you to commit to memory. Write this verse on an index card and take it with you throughout the day. Reflect on it as you drive in the car or wait for a bus or train. Let the verse become part of the inventory of Scriptures that guide your life.

Hebrews 4:12 says that "the word of God is alive and active. Sharper than any double-edged sword, it penetrates even to dividing soul and spirit, joints and marrow; it judges the thoughts and attitudes of the heart." Those of us who desire to follow Christ have chosen to base our decisions and lifestyles on the living and active sword of the Word of God.

The teachings of Scripture are not always easy. We don't usually like to have our thoughts and attitudes challenged. By embarking on this study, you have made the brave choice to journey closer to God's heart of love for all people. It will transform your life.

As you begin this study, pray that the Lord will give you an open heart to hear what he is saying to you personally through the Word. Pray for a willingness to be challenged by Scripture and for wisdom to know what God is calling you to as a result of this study. Ask him to give you a heart of compassion for the poor.

Compassion in
the Old Testament

WEEK
1

There are many hundreds of verses of Scripture that speak about poverty and justice. How many times does God need to express deep concern for the poor before we recognize how important they are to him?

This week, we will be studying some of the Old Testament passages of Scripture that help us understand God's heart of compassion for the poor.

There Should Be No Poor among You

"Didn't Jesus say in Matthew 26:11 that we would always have the poor with us?" People ask me this question often, and I think I know what they are implying.

If even Jesus acknowledged we would always be surrounded by poor people, doesn't that kind of let us off the hook? Shouldn't we acknowledge there is really nothing we can do to fundamentally change the plight of the poor? We might help an isolated person here or there temporarily; but if poverty is inevitable, why bother? We can drive by and drop off sandwiches to show our compassion or deposit a dollar or two in someone's outstretched cup, but certainly our little gestures will never really change anything. Even Jesus acknowledged that!

Did Jesus teach that we should tolerate poverty because it is just the way things are? Is poverty so inevitable that there's nothing we can do to alleviate the problem?

Today we examine the Old Testament passage Jesus may have been quoting when he said the poor would always be with us.

1. Pray for God's light to reveal the meaning of the Scripture and commit before the Lord to be willing to listen and obey.

2. Read Deuteronomy 15:4–11. In verse 4, the Lord says, "There should be no poor among you," and in verse 11 he says, "There will

always be poor people in the land." How do you account for this seeming contradiction?

3. Verse 4 indicates that "there should be no poor among you, for in the land the LORD your God is giving you to possess as your inheritance, he will richly bless you." In what ways have you been blessed?

4. What is required of those who have been blessed in their actions toward the poor (vv. 7–10)?

5. What do these verses say about the attitude we are to have as we lend and give to the poor?

6. The poor are often referred to in this passage as our brothers, our family. Isaiah 58:7 calls them our "own flesh and blood." How would it change your attitude toward the poor if you considered them to be your family?

7. Why do you think there are no admonitions directed toward the poor in Deuteronomy 15:4–11?

8. What specific admonitions are directed toward the Israelites as they enter the Promised Land?

Scripture Memory Verse

Deuteronomy 15:11: "There will always be poor people in the land. Therefore I command you to be openhanded toward your brothers and toward the poor and needy in your land."

DAY 2

Sharing the Harvest

God gave Israel many laws and commandments that ensured a safety net was in place for the needy. The poor weren't simply to be given handouts, but they were to be provided the opportunity to work alongside harvesters, picking up what was left behind. They were given productive work to do so they would not be reduced to begging to provide for their families. In this study, we will look at several Old Testament verses that lay out this dignifying system of compassionate care for the poor.

1. Pray that these verses of Scripture would be living and active in your heart and mind. Ask God to show you how these Scriptures can apply to your life.

2. Read Exodus 23:11 and Leviticus 23:22. These verses command the Israelites not to harvest to the edge of their fields, but to leave some of the crop for the poor to glean behind them. Imagine how different this experience of gleaning would be for the poor compared to being helpless recipients of charity. Can you think of modern-day examples of how the poor can be cared for in dignifying ways?

3. Read Ruth 2:3, 15–16. Boaz warned his workers not to embarrass or rebuke Ruth. This probably means the poor were sometimes treated in embarrassing or demeaning ways by the harvesters. What are some ways the poor are treated in condescending ways today?

4. Read Deuteronomy 14:28–29. What will be the outcome for those who use their resources to assure that the poor are satisfied?

5. Spend a few minutes in prayer. Ask God to show you dignifying ways to show care for the poor in your community.

Scripture Memory Verse

Proverbs 28:27: "He who gives to the poor will lack nothing, but he who closes his eyes to them receives many curses."

The Fast God Desires

Many who desire to follow Jesus and imitate the way he lived build spiritual disciplines into their lives to help them grow spiritually. We fast, pray, meditate, read our Bibles, meet in small groups with other Christians, and go to church. Without such practices, we tend to get off track spiritually and lose sight of God's work in the world and in us. Spiritual disciplines keep us spiritually healthy.

Similarly, the people addressed in our Scripture passage today had a sincere desire to be closer to God. According to the Lord, his people were doing many of the things that contribute to spiritual health, but they were frustrated in their efforts. They were praying and fasting to God, but to no avail. God seemed far away and unresponsive to their prayers.

God's response is surprising. He identified several actions that would bring them into right relationship with him and others. If his people would practice these disciplines, then he would hear and answer their prayers. God would heal them, guide them, and meet their needs. They would become like a well watered garden, like a spring whose waters never fail.

1. Pray that the Scripture reading today will help you learn what is important to God and how showing compassion to the poor can affect your life.

2. Read Isaiah 58:2–12. Have you ever felt like God was far away? Describe what that was like.

3. What spiritual disciplines do you practice to stay on track in your personal relationship with Christ?

4. How would you describe the people referred to in verses 2–5?

5. What actions characterize the fast that God requires (vv. 6–7)?

6. When Christians talk about spiritual disciplines, which ones usually come to mind?

7. Have the actions you listed in question 5 above been taught to you as spiritual disciplines? If not, why do you think that is?

8. List the results promised to those who care for the poor (vv. 8–12).

9. Are any results promised for the poor from the practices listed in verses 6–7? Why or why not?

10. Review the actions you listed in question 5. Take a few moments to pray and reflect upon your own spiritual disciplines. What might God be inviting you to include among your regular practices?

Scripture Memory Verse

Isaiah 58:8: "Then your light will break forth like the dawn, and your healing will quickly appear."

DAY 4

Josiah's Repentance

Kay Warren tells the story of a life-changing experience that started when she read an article about the twelve million HIV/AIDS orphans in Africa.[1] Her husband, Rick, was tentative in his support of his wife's new cause, until he, too, experienced a breakthrough after visiting Africa and seeing firsthand the devastating impact of poverty and AIDS. He was driven to reexamine Scripture with new eyes, and what he found humbled him.

> I found those [two thousand] verses on the poor. How did I miss that? I went to Bible college, two seminaries, and I got a doctorate. How did I miss God's compassion for the poor? I was not seeing all the purposes of God.
>
> The church is the body of Christ. The hands and feet have been amputated, and we're just a big mouth, known more for what we're against. . . . [Warren prayed,] "God, would you use me to reattach the hands and the feet to the body of Christ, so that the whole church cares about the whole gospel in a whole new way—through the local church?"[2]

Josiah was just eight years old when he began to reign over Judah. Josiah's grandfather, Manasseh, and his father, Amon, had allowed the country to fall away from God and into corruption. When Josiah was sixteen years old, he began to seek the Lord. He tore down the Asherah poles that were used to worship other gods, and he purged Judah and Jerusalem of the incense altars and idols. When he was twenty-six, he asked the religious leaders to repair and restore the temple. In it, they found scrolls of the Pentateuch, the law of God. They rushed their newfound treasure to Josiah and read God's Word to him. Hilkiah the high priest consulted Huldah the prophetess who warned that calamity would come to the land if the Word of God was not obeyed. When Josiah heard the Word, he tore his robe, put ashes on his head, and repented.

Later, Jeremiah would say about King Josiah: "'He defended the cause of the poor and needy, and so all went well. Is that not what it means to know me?' declares the LORD" (Jer. 22:16).

1. Pray that the Spirit will reveal to you Scriptures about the poor that may have been lost in recent church history due to selective focus and neglect.

2. Read 2 Kings 22:8–11. When the Word of God was read to Josiah, he tore his robe in repentance. What do you think he was thinking and feeling?

3. Why do you think he felt he needed to repent?

4. In *The Invisible*, I mention that Scriptures about caring for the poor had been largely ignored or spiritualized away in many of the churches I attended. Like in Josiah's day, entire passages of Scripture seem to have been lost (pp. 106–107). Why do you think some church leaders do not preach or teach about the poor?

5. Read Jeremiah 22:11–16. Jeremiah said that Josiah became known for defending the cause of the poor and needy and then quoted the Lord as saying, "Is that not what it means to know me?" (v. 16). How is defending the cause of the poor and needy connected to knowing God?

6. Josiah repented when the Word of God was read to him. Repentance is asking forgiveness for sin, including neglect, and turning around or changing direction. God doesn't wield a club over our heads to get us to care for the poor, but he invites us to live lives that are "right and just." Take a few moments to pray and let God know that you desire to grow in your capacity to defend "the cause of the poor and needy" (v. 16).

Scripture Memory Verse

Jeremiah 22:16: "He defended the cause of the poor and needy, and so all went well. 'Is that not what it means to know me?' declares the LORD."

Notes

1. Timothy C. Morgan, "Purpose Driven in Rwanda," *Christianity Today* (October 2005): accessed March 9, 2011, http://www.christianity today.com/ct/2005/ october/17.32.html.

2. Ibid., http://www.christianitytoday.com/ct/2005/october/17.32.html? start=2.

God's Commitment to Compassion

In Ezekiel 34, God expressed anger toward shepherds who were not taking care of their flock. God reprimanded them in verse 4, saying, "You have not strengthened the weak or healed the sick or bound up the injured. You have not brought back the strays or searched for the lost. You have ruled them harshly and brutally." In verse 16, God declared, "I will search for the lost and bring back the strays. I will bind up the injured and strengthen the weak." He continued, "Therefore this is what the Sovereign LORD says to them: See, I myself will judge between the fat sheep and the lean sheep. Because you shove with flank and shoulder, butting all the weak sheep with your horns until you have driven them away" (vv. 20–21).

God was so committed to compassionate care for the weak, sick, and injured that he would step in and care for them if others didn't. Yet it is clear from Ezekiel 34 that God positioned shepherds for the weak and injured and expected the shepherds to search for them and look after them. Today, we will study the verses at the end of Ezekiel 34 that describe a beautiful covenant that God makes with those who are abandoned by society.

1. Pray that God will reveal the meaning of the Scripture today. Pray for openness to receive any word God might have for you personally.

2. Read Ezekiel 34:25–31. A covenant is a promise. Make a list of all that God promises to do for those who suffer the neglect of their established caretakers.

3. Every year, hundreds of thousands of women and children are abducted, deceived, seduced, or sold into forced prostitution. According to this passage, what does God promise to do for them?

4. What will they know as a result of God's act of freeing them?

5. What does God promise for those who suffer famine?

6. What will they know as a result of God's care for them?

7. Take a few minutes to pray and ask God to give you his heart of compassion for those who have been cast aside, abused, and neglected by those who should be caring for them. Ask God how he would like you to respond.

Scripture Memory Verse

Ezekiel 34:16: "I will search for the lost and bring back the strays. I will bind up the injured and strengthen the weak, but the sleek and the strong I will destroy. I will shepherd the flock with justice."

Compassion in the Old Testament

GROUP DISCUSSION GUIDE

This week we studied Old Testament passages of Scripture that reveal God's compassion for the poor. God established guidelines that would ensure the poor were cared for with dignity. The prophet Isaiah recorded God's message about the kind of fast God desires. We also read about Josiah, who repented of his neglect and disobedience to the commands of God and chose to defend the cause of the poor and needy. God cares deeply about the weak and injured and will take action if those entrusted with their care are negligent.

1. Open your group meeting in prayer, thanking God for the presence of the Holy Spirit and ask for guidance.

2. Why do you think people are hesitant to talk about poverty or engage in relationships across socioeconomic lines?

3. How do you feel when you are asked to give to the poor? What reservations do you have and why?

4. What have you experienced in your life that has softened your heart toward the poor?

5. How did God's commands assure that the poor would be cared for with dignity?

6. According to the Scripture passages we read this week, what are the personal benefits that God's people experience when we care for the poor?

7. Share with the group how you have personally experienced the joy of caring for others.

8. Where do the poor live in your neighborhood?

9. How might our group get involved in caring for their needs?

10. Spend time in prayer together. Pray for the ministries in your area that care for the poor.

The Example of Jesus

WEEK
2

People who are serious about following Jesus will inevitably follow him to the poor. Jesus was a strong advocate for compassionate care for the poor. He taught and modeled it consistently throughout his life by the way he entered the world, the family he was born into, the people he chose to share his life with, his opening mission statement, and his death on the cross. This week, we will study how Jesus advocated for compassion for the poor through the example of his life and his teaching. We will consider what it means for us to live the way Jesus did, to defend the cause of the poor, and lay down our lives for people who are weak, injured, and needy.

His Incarnation

Incarnation is a theological word that means Jesus came to earth in the flesh, as a human being. Jesus had it all: riches, power, and authority. Everything was his and at his command. His power was so great, it exploded into stars and planets. His very presence was overwhelming. Everything around him was moved to hushed silence or rocked by tempestuous storms. Wild winds, crashing waves—he created it all with just a word. He commanded everything. He ruled. He was intimate with God. He was equal with God. He was (and is) God.

Jesus willingly left all of that power and position behind to become the most vulnerable human being imaginable, a naked baby born to a young mother in a poor working-class family. That was how God chose to enter the world in a physical form. Jesus was incarnated; he put on flesh and came to live among us.

1. Pray for God's light to reveal the meaning of the incarnation of Jesus and how you can "incarnate" Jesus through your earthly body today.

2. Read Philippians 2:6–8. Why is it significant that Jesus came to earth humbly, as a servant, rather than riding in a chariot to take a position on a kingly throne?

3. Read Luke 2:22–24. Forty days after the birth of a first son, the boy's parents were required by the Law to offer a sacrifice for his

dedication. If the family could not afford a lamb, they were allowed to bring a pair of doves or pigeons. Joseph and Mary could only afford the birds. What does this tell us about the economic class of Jesus' earthly family?

4. Read Matthew 8:20. Jesus identified with the poor wanderers on earth that have no place to lay their heads. Why do you think this was important to Jesus?

5. In *The Invisible*, I recommended that we follow Jesus by practicing the breakthrough of presence—to simply be with people to listen, observe, and let our hearts be touched (ch. 7). Often we feel we need to bring an agenda or some tangible resource. But what people need more is to be heard and understood. There are relatively safe ways you can come alongside people who struggle by volunteering at shelters and ministry centers that care for the impoverished. Jesus modeled the breakthrough of presence by coming to live on earth with us. He spent time with people in conversation. How can you follow Jesus in coming alongside people who are destitute and needy?

6. Instead of grasping for power, Jesus was willing to take the form of a servant. How can you become more incarnate to the poor in your community? How can you serve them?

7. Take time to pray and ask God to reveal opportunities for you to be his hands and feet among the poor today.

Scripture Memory Verses

Philippians 2:5–8: "Your attitude should be the same as that of Christ Jesus: Who, being in very nature God, did not consider equality with God something to be grasped, but made himself nothing, taking the very nature of a servant, being made in human likeness. And being found in appearance as a man, he humbled himself and became obedient to death—even death on a cross!"

DAY 2

His Mission

At the beginning of Jesus' public ministry, he entered the temple and asked for a scroll of the book of Isaiah. He unrolled it to Isaiah 61 and read the first two verses. Then he rolled up the scroll and gave it back to the attendant and said, "Today this scripture is fulfilled in your hearing" (Luke 4:21).

Jesus had a clear mission on earth. He knew what he was sent to do. Today you will read about his proclamation and reflect upon the mission that God has for us.

1. Pray for God's light to understand the mission of Christ on earth, and ask him to reveal to you the good works he has prepared for you to do.

2. Read Luke 4:14–21. List the things Jesus was sent to accomplish according to verses 18–19.

3. Read Matthew 11:2–5. While in prison, John asked his disciples to ask Jesus if he was the true Messiah or if they should look for another. What accomplishments did Jesus use to validate the fact that he was the Son of God?

4. What might we expect to be indications that Jesus' work is still being carried out by his followers today?

5. Ephesians 2:10 indicates that we have been created to do good works that have been prepared in advance for us to do. What good works do you think God has planned for you to do?

6. Take a few minutes to reflect on your God-given gifts and abilities and on how God might want to use you to carry out Jesus' mission on earth. Pray that God will reveal to you the good works you have been uniquely designed to accomplish. If you have time, write a mission statement for yourself.

Scripture Memory Verse

Ephesians 2:10: "For we are God's workmanship, created in Christ Jesus to do good works, which God prepared in advance for us to do."

His Miracles

Jesus performed many miracles while on earth. His miracles were not egotistical displays of his power. Jesus performed miracles that healed people, fed them, raised them from the dead, and brought them new life. Today, we will study several passages that describe some of the miracles of Jesus and look at what motivated him to act on behalf of the people involved.

1. Pray for God's light to reveal the meaning of the Scripture, and commit to the Lord to be willing to listen and obey.

2. Read Matthew 4:23–24. These verses describe the types of people who were drawn to Jesus as he was preparing to preach his famous Sermon on the Mount message. Sometimes known as the Beatitudes, the sermon started with the statement, "Blessed are the poor" (Matt. 5:3). List the struggles of the people who gathered around Jesus.

3. How did Jesus respond to their needs?

4. Read Matthew 14:15–21. What did the disciples ask Jesus to do with the crowd of hungry people in verse 15?

5. What did Jesus tell them to do in verse 16?

6. Read John 9:1–12. The disciples wanted to know who to blame for the man being born blind. What was Jesus' answer?

7. Why do you think many of us want to know who is to blame when we find people in distress?

8. How have you seen the work of God displayed in the lives of people who are born into difficult circumstances?

9. Take a few minutes to pray. Ask God to show you where his work is being displayed in tough places.

Scripture Memory Verse

John 9:3: "'Neither this man nor his parents sinned,' said Jesus, 'but this happened so that the work of God might be displayed in his life.'"

DAY
4

His Relationships

Jesus went out of his way to befriend people who struggled. When the Jews who had been exiled to Babylon returned to their land, they found it occupied by a group of mixed-race Samaritans. These Samaritans were despised by the Jews and were carefully avoided. Today, we will look at three examples of how Jesus crossed the established boundaries of his day and reached out to social outcasts.

1. Pray for God's light to understand the relevance of the types of relationships Jesus developed and the wisdom to know how to cross socioeconomic barriers to show Christ's love.

2. Read Matthew 11:19. Jesus so closely associated with alcoholics and overeaters that he was accused by his critics of being a drunkard and glutton. Who are some modern-day outcasts you might have a difficult time associating with for fear of being accused as one of them?

3. How many relationships do you have with people who are struggling with addictions?

4. Read Luke 7:36–39. Why do you think the Pharisees were concerned when they saw that Jesus let a woman with a sinful reputation touch him?

5. What was Jesus more concerned about?

6. Read John 4:4–29. Most Jews went out of their way to bypass Samaria, yet Jesus *had* to go through Samaria. Why?

7. What social or religious barriers did Jesus cross in talking with the woman at the well?

8. What reaction did the disciples have when they saw Jesus interacting with the Samaritan woman?

9. What was the outcome of Jesus' conversation with the woman?

10. Take a few minutes to pray. Ask God to reveal to you if there are any social outcasts who are in need of your friendship and attention.

Scripture Memory Verse

John 4:14: "But whoever drinks the water I give him will never thirst. Indeed, the water I give him will become in him a spring of water welling up to eternal life."

DAY 5

His Teaching

Jesus not only modeled compassion for the poor, but he also taught it regularly. We have already studied his declaration in Luke 4 that his mission was to preach good news to the poor, to proclaim freedom for the prisoners and recovery of sight to the blind, and to release the oppressed. Today, we will look at some of his words as he preached and proclaimed good news to the poor.

1. Pray for God's light to reveal the meaning of Christ's teaching, and ask God to help you to listen and obey God's Word as it speaks to you today.

2. Read Matthew 25:31–46. How can we show love to Jesus? List the actions Jesus listed.

3. Ephesians 2:8–9 makes it clear that we don't earn our salvation by the good works that we do, yet these verses in Matthew 25 seem to indicate that those of us who know Jesus will be actively involved in loving Jesus through caring for "the least of these" (Matt. 25:45). Caring for those who are hungry, thirsty, naked, strangers, sick, and in prison is core to the DNA of true Christians. As Jeremiah wrote about Josiah (Jer. 22:16), defending the cause of the poor and needy is what it means to know God. According to Matthew 25:46, what will be the outcome for those who don't care for the poor?

4. Read Matthew 23:23–24. What upsets Jesus?

5. What words did Jesus use to describe those who neglect justice, mercy, and faithfulness?

6. Read Luke 11:39–41. What do you think Jesus meant when he said the Pharisees cleaned the outside of the cup and dish but were full of greed and wickedness on the inside?

7. What did Jesus say would make the inside of the cup clean?

8. Take a few minutes to pray and ask God to show you how you can love Jesus by caring for "the least of these."

Scripture Memory Verse

Matthew 25:40: "The King will reply, 'I tell you the truth, whatever you did for one of the least of these brothers of mine, you did for me.'"

The Example of Jesus

GROUP DISCUSSION GUIDE

This week we examined the life of Jesus and saw how he went out of his way to cross boundaries of race and class to draw near to social outcasts. Jesus was moved with compassion for those who were "harassed and helpless, like sheep without a shepherd" (Matt. 9:36). We looked at his example through the incarnation, his mission, his miracles, his relationships, and his teaching.

1. Open your group meeting in prayer, thanking God for the presence of the Holy Spirit. Ask for guidance.

2. What were some of the highlights of this week's study for you?

3. Ask members of the group to volunteer to read some or all of the following Scriptures. As the passages are read, write your thoughts.

- Matthew 4:23–24

- Matthew 8:20

- Matthew 11:2–5

- Matthew 11:19

- Matthew 14:15–21

- Matthew 23:23–24
- Matthew 25:31–46
- Luke 2:22–24
- Luke 4:14–21
- Luke 7:36–39
- Luke 11:39–42
- John 4:4–29
- John 9:1–12
- Philippians 2:6–8

4. Share with the group some of your thoughts from the above Scriptures. What themes emerge?

5. If Jesus was living on earth today, where do you think we would find him? What would he be doing?

6. Ephesians 2:10 states that God has prepared good works for us to do. Share with the group your thoughts this week about what those good works are for you.

7. What ministries or organizations do you know about that are carrying out the actions that Jesus listed in Matthew 25?

8. How can your group assist those organizations in their missions?

9. Spend time in prayer for one another and ask God to give discernment and direction for each one in your group to what good works he or she is being called. Ask God for the courage to step out in faith to be the hands and feet of Jesus to a hurting world.

The Model of the Early Church

A secular sociologist named Rodney Stark wrote a book entitled, *The Rise of Christianity: How the Obscure, Marginal Jesus Movement Became the Dominant Religious Force in the Western World in a Few Centuries*. Stark's thesis was that Christianity grew because it improved the quality of life in the community and cared for the poor.[1]

Women were not valued during the period of the start of the early church. An archeological dig actually discovered a sewer line clogged with infant baby girls. As they were discarded into the sewer or tossed to the street to die, Christians joined a movement to stand up against the killing of infants and organized to retrieve rejected baby girls and nurse them to health.[2] Many of these girls grew up to be Christ followers.

When young women gathered at the local market to chat, many would complain that their husbands had been unfaithful. The Christian women would tell the other women about their loving and faithful husbands. Soon all the women wanted to have Christian husbands who would honor and respect them, and they sought them out.

When health plagues ravaged the cities and people were dying, those with resources would flee to safety in the rural areas until the plague passed. The Christians stayed and cared for the sick. They found that with minimal nursing care, many of the diseased could be saved. Many of the grateful recipients of this compassion embraced the love of Christ as well. A few centuries later, Christianity was the dominant religion of the Roman world.

This week, we will be studying the model of the early church to see what we can learn about the foundation of this community of faith. We will look for ways the modern church may have veered off track and discuss how our churches can rise again to be the compassionate body of Christ among the hurting in our communities.

Notes

1. Rodney Stark, *The Rise of Christianity: How the Obscure, Marginal Jesus Movement Became the Dominant Religious Force in the Western World in a Few Centuries* (Princeton, N.J.: Princeton University Press, 1996).

2. Ibid., 118.

The Church at Antioch

The followers of Jesus were first called Christians at Antioch. Antioch was a very densely populated city and a center of government and civilization. In an age when there were no high-rise buildings, it is estimated that Antioch was home to roughly seventy-five thousand inhabitants per square mile or 117 per acre. This represents a higher population density than some of our largest, modern cities. Living conditions were bleak. Human and animal waste muddied the streets causing filth that spawned chronic health conditions. Life expectancy at birth was less than thirty years. It was in this chaotic environment that the good news of Jesus began to thrive. Christians were known for their compassionate care of the poor and the castaways.

Today, we will study two passages that describe the church at Antioch to try to discover what may have caused their message of the gospel of Jesus to be so readily embraced.

1. Pray for God to speak to you through the Scriptures today. Ask him to help you understand how to apply the Scripture to your situation.

2. Read Acts 11:19–30. What caused the believers to move from Jerusalem to Antioch?

3. How has God used difficulties in your life to produce a greater good?

4. Read John 16:2, 7. Jesus had predicted that his followers would suffer persecution after he left. He also made the surprising statement that it would be good for them that he left. Why?

5. What evidence is there in the Acts 11:19–30 that the Holy Spirit was indeed with the believers?

6. What evidence have you seen in your life that the Holy Spirit is guiding you?

7. How did the church at Antioch respond to the news that a famine was coming to Judea?

8. Guided by the Holy Spirit, the church at Antioch brought the good news of Jesus into a bleak and chaotic environment. How would your community be different if your church did not exist?

9. One of the keys to avoiding burnout in ministry is to be led by the Spirit rather than driven by need. Spend some time in prayer and ask the Holy Spirit to guide you to know how you can serve Christ today.

Scripture Memory Verse

Acts 1:8: "But you will receive power when the Holy Spirit comes on you; and you will be my witnesses in Jerusalem, and in all Judea and Samaria, and to the ends of the earth."

The Early Church and the Poor

We live in an age of unprecedented consumerism and self-indulgence. The public storage industry is booming as Americans buy more space to store all of the stuff we own. We have bigger houses, drive more cars, and eat out more often than ever.

Smith, Emerson, and Snell, in their book *Passing the Plate: Why American Christians Don't Give Away More Money*, write, "Materialistic consumption has become a nearly inescapable way of life in the United States . . . the dominance of mass consumerism works powerfully and in many ways against American Christians freely and liberally giving away significant proportions of their incomes . . . as most of their religious traditions call them to do. The first and perhaps most formidable rival to generous voluntary financial giving of American Christians, then, aiding and abetting any of their natural human tendencies toward selfishness and stinginess, is America's institutionalized mass consumerism."[1]

Today we will see how the early church viewed material possessions and will reflect upon our own habits of consumption and generosity.

1. Pray for God's light to reveal the meaning of the Scripture, and commit to learn how you can use material possessions to care for the poor.

2. Read Acts 2:42–47 and 4:32–35. List the characteristics of the early church described in these passages of Scripture.

3. How did they view material possessions?

4. What was the result of this sharing of possessions?

5. Psalm 24:1 tells us, "The earth is the LORD's, and everything in it." In Psalm 50:9–10, God says, "I have no need of a bull from your stall or of goats from your pens, for every animal of the forest is mine, and the cattle on a thousand hills." Read pages 159–171 of *The Invisible*. What does it mean to be a steward of someone else's property?

6. Jesus said in Matthew 6:21, "For where your treasure is, there your heart will be also." How will sharing your possessions with the poor affect your level of compassion for them?

7. What keeps you from being more generous?

8. If you have children, what do you think your children are learning from you about material possessions?

9. What examples do you have of God using children to teach you about stewardship?

10. Take some time to reflect upon your stewardship of the material possessions God has entrusted to your care. Are there steps you could take to become more generous?

Scripture Memory Verse

2 Corinthians 9:7: "Each man should give what he has decided in his heart to give, not reluctantly or under compulsion, for God loves a cheerful giver."

Note

1. Christian Smith, Michael O. Emerson, and Patricia Snell, *Passing the Plate: Why American Christians Don't Give Away More Money* (New York: Oxford University Press, 2008), 176.

The Apostle Paul's Concern for the Poor

In the first century after Christ's death, the apostle Paul traveled throughout Cappadocia, Asia, and Macedonia, establishing and visiting churches. He wrote thirteen letters called Epistles to these churches. They are books in the New Testament of the Bible. Paul was very concerned that these early churches continued to care for the poor like the church of Acts 2. Today, we will look at some of Paul's teaching about giving to assist the poor.

1. Pray for God's light to reveal the meaning of the Scripture, and commit before the Lord to be willing to listen and obey what God tells you do through his Word.

2. Read Galatians 2:9–10. What was the one thing that the pillars of the early church, James, Peter, and John, asked of Paul and Barnabas when they were given the right hand of fellowship to bring the gospel to the Gentiles?

3. How did Paul feel about this request?

4. Read 1 Corinthians 16:1–3. What did Paul instruct the people of the churches of Corinth and Galatia to do?

5. Where were these gifts going to be sent?

6. Read Acts 11:28 and Romans 15:26. What were the saints in Jerusalem experiencing?

7. What are some similar devastating circumstances throughout the world that might be forcing people into poverty?

8. Who, like Paul, is organizing on their behalf?

9. Read 2 Corinthians 8:1–15. What do we learn about the Macedonian churches?

10. Was everyone supposed to give the same amount? How was the amount to be determined?

11. What principles about generous giving can you glean from this passage?

12. Pray through the principles you listed above and ask God to help you to grow in the grace of giving.

Scripture Memory Verse

Luke 6:38: "Give, and it will be given to you. A good measure, pressed down, shaken together and running over, will be poured into your lap. For with the measure you use, it will be measured to you."

Faith and Works

The Holy Spirit guided the early church to bring the good news of forgiveness through faith in Christ while they also cared for the physical needs of the poor. Faith and works went hand in hand as they carried out the commands of Jesus to love the Lord with heart, soul, mind, and strength and to love their neighbors as themselves. Today, we will look at this message of showing the love of God through both faith and good works.

1. Pray for God's light to reveal the meaning of the Scripture, and commit before the Lord to be willing to listen to and obey what God speaks to you through the Holy Spirit.

2. Read Ephesians 2:8–10. Our salvation is a gift from God which comes to us through faith in Christ and does not depend upon our good works. What is the purpose God has for each of us?

3. Read 1 John 3:14–18. How do we know that we have passed from death to life?

4. What does 1 John 3:16–17 say will be the outcome of our lives if we have experienced the love of God?

5. Read James 2:14–17. Is it possible to have true Christian faith and not care about the poor?

6. Read Galatians 5:5–6. Paul addressed members of the church at Galatia who were disputing about whether it was necessary for the Gentiles to become circumcised like the Jews in order to be saved. What did Paul say was the only thing that mattered?

7. How have you experienced the love of God through people of faith?

8. Take a few minutes to thank God for the ways you have experienced love, and ask him to show you how you can express his love to people around you today.

Scripture Memory Verse

Ephesians 2:10: "For we are God's workmanship, created in Christ Jesus to do good works, which God prepared in advance for us to do."

DAY 5

The Church of Laodicea

Today, we are going to fast forward from A.D. 61, when Paul wrote the book of Colossians, to A.D. 95, when John penned a message from Christ to the church at Laodicea. Laodicea was less than fifteen miles from Colosse, and Paul instructed that his letter to the Colossians should also be read to the Laodiceans (Col. 4:16). By A.D. 95, Laodicea had become a center of trade, banking, and fashion. It was an important city because it was located at the crossroads of three main highways. The city developed and sold a type of glossy black wool that made the residents very wealthy.

The church had become corrupt, and Jesus had harsh words for them. Let's look at what led to their demise and see how God responded.

1. Pray for God's light to show you how to avoid the trap of the Laodiceans.

2. Read Revelation 3:14–19. God said that the church was neither hot nor cold, but lukewarm. According to verse 15, what did God know? What was the evidence that they were lukewarm?

3. God wished that they would be either hot or cold. Why would God prefer a cold church over a lukewarm one?

4. What was God going to do with them (v. 16)?

5. What were the people saying and believing that displeased God?

6. What situations in your life right now make it clear to you that you need God?

7. What might cause people to think they don't have any needs?

8. What did God say the Laodicean church had failed to realize?

9. It seems from this passage that it is possible to have material wealth and still be poor. How would you describe this kind of poverty?

10. What does God advise the church to do in verse 18?

11. According to verse 19, what does God do for people he loves?

12. The New International Version reads verse 19 as, "Be earnest, and repent." Another translation says, "Be diligent and turn from your indifference" (NLT). Is there anything that you may have become indifferent toward about which God might be calling you to repent?

Scripture Memory Verse

1 John 3:16: "This is how we know what love is: Jesus Christ laid down his life for us. And we ought to lay down our lives for our brothers."

The Model of the Early Church

GROUP DISCUSSION GUIDE

This week we learned about the early church and how its people expressed compassion for the poor. The early church clearly recognized how important this is. It was led by the Spirit to respond during times of calamity, and was known for its compassion.

1. Have someone open your group meeting in prayer, asking God to guide your conversation.

2. What were some of the major characteristics of the early church?

3. The early church suffered persecution. The suffering scattered the people to new locations and spread the good news of Jesus even more quickly. How has God used difficulties in your life or in the history of your church to produce a positive outcome?

4. The early church was guided by the Holy Spirit. Have you ever been led to do something by the whisper of the Holy Spirit?

5. The early church seemed to enjoy giving. How central is giving to the poor to your church ministry?

6. Discuss ways your church is engaging with the poor.

7. What factors might lead Christians to becoming indifferent to the needs of the poor?

8. What can you do to move your congregation to more meaningful engagement with the poor?

9. Spend time in prayer together. Ask God to lead your church and group by the Holy Spirit to know how you can apply principles from the passages studied this past week.

WEEK 4 Who Is My Neighbor?

In Luke 10:25–37, an attorney asked Jesus what he needed to do to inherit eternal life. Jesus responded to his question with a question of his own, asking him what was written in the Law. The attorney answered with a quote from Deuteronomy 6 that every practicing Jewish person would have known, both then and today. It is the Jewish Shema, an affirmation of faith that is recited on a daily basis, for both ordinary and special occasions.

The attorney replied, "Love the Lord your God with all your heart and with all your soul and with all your strength and with all your mind." Then he added another commandment, from Leviticus 19:18, "and love your neighbor as yourself" (Luke 10:27).

"'You have answered correctly,'" Jesus replied. "'Do this and you will live'" (v. 28).

Luke said the man wanted to justify himself, so he asked Jesus the question, "And who is my neighbor?" (v. 29).

Jesus answered him with a story. A man was walking along the road to Jericho when he was mugged. He was robbed, stripped, beaten, and left to die. Two religious leaders passed down the road. Seeing the mugged man in his distress, they passed by on the other side. A Samaritan man went to where the man was and felt pity for him. He bandaged the man's wounds, put him on his own donkey, took him to the nearest shelter, and paid for his rehabilitation. This man, said Jesus, was the neighbor who understood what it meant to love.

This week, we will look at Scriptures that expand on this man's response of love for the broken. We will try to discover what it means today to love God and love people, to love our neighbors as ourselves.

The Good Samaritan

The story of the good Samaritan is a familiar one. Jesus used it to explain what is essential for followers of Jesus. While Matthew and Mark say the attorney's question was about the most important commandments, Luke said his question was about what he needed to do to inherent eternal life. Either way, Jesus said that how we love God and how we show love to our neighbor is a key part of what it means to follow him and keep his commands.

1. Pray for God to reveal the meaning of the Scriptures you read today. Ask him to help you grow in love for your neighbor.

2. Read Luke 10:25–37; Mark 12:28–34; and Matthew 22:35–40. Matthew, Mark, and Luke all tell the same story, but from slightly different perspectives. Why do you think the attorney asked Jesus to explain what was most important?

3. Have you ever wished you could boil down life into one or two meaningful codes to live by? What are some of the principles you have chosen to guide your life?

4. Remember that the Samaritans were despised by the Jews. Why is it significant that Jesus chose the good neighbor in the story to be a Samaritan?

5. The priest and the Levite were religious leaders. How did they react when they saw the mugged man?

6. What might be some reasons why the priest and Levite avoided getting involved?

7. Have you ever avoided getting involved with broken people? Why or why not?

8. The Samaritan man "came where the man was" (Luke 10:33). In a previous study, we talked about the breakthrough of presence—going to places where you will be in contact with the poor. Where can you go in your community to be near people who are struggling and broken?

9. The Samaritan man did what he could to bandage the injured man's wounds and then put him on his own donkey and brought him to the nearest shelter. What ministries or organizations care for hurting people in your community? Where would you take someone who is struggling with addiction, unplanned pregnancy, hunger, or domestic abuse?

10. Take a few minutes to pray and ask God to let you know how you can cross the road to be near people in need.

Scripture Memory Verse

Luke 10:27: "'Love the Lord your God with all your heart and with all your soul and with all your strength and with all your mind'; and, 'Love your neighbor as yourself.'"

DAY
2

What Is Compassion?

The Samaritan man went to be near the mugged man. When he saw the man in his distress he "felt compassion" (NLT). The word *compassion* is Latin and means "to bear with" or "to suffer with." Compassion allows one to feel, understand, and respond to the suffering of others.

The Greek word for compassion is *splagchnizomai*. The *splagchnon*—the abdomen, womb, or bowels—was considered to be the seat of one's strongest emotions. To have *splagcnivzomai* was to be moved in the *splagchnon*. Both Jesus and the Samaritan man in Jesus' story were moved by compassion when they saw people in need.

When I heard the meaning of this Greek word for compassion, I was reminded of my experience after the birth of my children. When a newborn baby cries, the mother has an immediate physiological reaction. Her abdomen instinctively and often painfully contracts, and she feels a strong compulsion to reach out and draw the crying baby into her arms. It is automatic and powerful. Those of you who have given birth have experienced this.

The same, I believe, is true for all who have within them the compassionate heart of God. We cannot resist the cry of human need. It reaches into the deepest parts of us and requires that we respond. It is automatic, and the call to action is powerful. That is why the practice of presence, just going to where hurting people are, will change your life if you know Jesus. You will be compelled to action.

1. Pray for God's light as you study the word *compassion* in the Scripture today. Ask him to help you grow in your ability to suffer with people in pain.

2. Read Luke 10:33. What did the Samaritan man feel when he saw that the mugged man had been beaten and was lying helpless at the side of the road?

3. Read Matthew 9:35–36. What was Jesus doing as he traveled through the towns and villages?

4. What did Jesus feel when he saw the crowds that were harassed and helpless, like sheep without a shepherd?

5. The same Greek word that was used for what Jesus felt when he saw the crowds is used for the Samaritan when he saw the mugged man. Describe a situation when you have felt deep compassion.

6. What actions have you been moved to take when you have felt compassion?

7. Read Psalm 34:18. God "is close to the brokenhearted." Perhaps when we come alongside the brokenhearted, we come near to God as well. Describe a time when you experienced God by coming alongside someone who was brokenhearted.

8. Spend some time in prayer. Ask God to grow your heart of compassion.

Scripture Memory Verse

Matthew 9:36: "When he saw the crowds, he had compassion on them, because they were harassed and helpless, like sheep without a shepherd."

DAY 3
Possessions and Wealth

Many of us struggle with our responsibility to the poor. Is it OK for me to have what I have and live where I live? Is giving money an appropriate response, and if so, how much and to whom? Must I, like the rich young ruler of Scripture, give all I own to the poor in order to follow Jesus? Should I be selling everything and moving into an inner-city ghetto or to India or Africa? Is God pleased with how I am living? What, if anything, that I do will make a difference?

A woman once approached me after a presentation and said, "I make a lot of money. I feel guilty. I want to help, but I just don't know how. My job keeps me very busy, and I don't have much time to volunteer. What should I do?"

I assured her that she didn't need to leave her high-paying job to engage with the poor. In fact, I believe strongly that God gives certain people the ability to create wealth. Investing her wealth to open doors of opportunity for struggling ministries among the poor could be the calling God has placed on her life.

Today, we will read verses from Scripture that shed light on how we can love our neighbors with our wealth.

1. Pray for God's light as you reflect on your use of material possessions, and ask him to show you if there are any changes you

are being asked to make in obedience to the prompting of the Holy Spirit.

2. Read 1 Timothy 6:17–19. Paul instructed his young mentee Timothy to command people who are rich not to be arrogant or put their hope in wealth. Why might people who are wealthy become arrogant?

3. Do you ever worry about your finances? What assurance does Luke 12:22–32 provide?

4. Read Mark 10:25. Why might it be difficult for rich people to enter the kingdom of God?

5. According to Ezekiel 16:49, what was the sin of Sodom?

6. Read Deuteronomy 8:18. Where does the ability to create wealth come from?

7. Read Matthew 6:20–21. How do we store up treasure in heaven?

8. If your heart follows your treasure, how might giving to the poor increase your level of compassion?

9. Spend a few minutes in prayer. Ask God to release you from worry and for the Spirit to guide you as you make decisions about your finances.

Scripture Memory Verse

Matthew 6:20: "Store up for yourselves treasures in heaven, where moth and rust do not destroy, and where thieves do not break in and steal."

Responding to Panhandlers

Panhandlers seem to bombard those in the city. They wash our car windshields at the gas station and then come to our windows expecting payments. They cling to ragtag cardboard signs and approach us with forlorn faces. Some are in obvious need. They truly are blind, missing legs, or sitting in wheelchairs, holding dirty cups.

What should we do?

As the leader of an organization that specializes in ministry among the homeless, let me give you my expert opinion: I don't know!

I think God gives us these dilemmas to cause us to rely on the compassion of Christ he has implanted in our hearts. Coming face-to-face with someone who asks us for money is an opportunity to be led by the Spirit instead of being driven by need, guilt, obligation, or the desire to bolster our own ego as a generous person. There is no simple answer.

Today, we will look at some passages of Scripture that will guide our actions as we interact with people on the street who ask us for money.

1. Pray for God's light as you study the Scripture today. Ask him to guide you to know how you should respond to panhandlers.

2. How do you typically respond to panhandlers?

3. Read Luke 6:30. Jesus said to give to everyone who asks. Can you think of situations in which giving cash might not be the best way to respond? Why?

4. What are ways—other than cash—that you can give to someone who asks of you?

5. Read Matthew 10:16. What does it mean to be both shrewd and innocent when responding to panhandlers?

6. Read James 2:13. How might this verse influence your decisions about how to respond to panhandlers?

7. Read Acts 3:6. How did Peter respond when he was asked for money?

8. The Samaritan man took the mugged man to a place where he could experience recovery and paid for his stay. What ministries in your community can you support to assist in the recovery of those who face difficult circumstances?

9. I've suggested that we should be led by the Spirit rather than driven by need. Describe a time when the Spirit led you to do an act of compassion for someone in need.

10. Take a few minutes to pray. Ask the Holy Spirit to guide you to know how to respond when people ask you for help.

Scripture Memory Verse

Luke 6:30: "Give to everyone who asks you, and if anyone takes what belongs to you, do not demand it back."

Investing in the Kingdom

Jesus tells a story of a man who gave ten of his servants one *mina* each, the equivalent of three months' wages, and instructed them to put the money to work while he was away. When he came back from his journey, the master sent for the servants to whom he had given the money "to find out what they had gained with it" (Luke 19:15).

One of the servants had wisely invested the money and had received a tenfold return! Let's say in today's terms the servant was given twelve thousand dollars. When the master returned from his journey, this faithful servant had turned the twelve thousand dollars into one hundred twenty thousand dollars! You can imagine the delight of the master! He calls him good and probably pats him on the back as he says, "Well done!" (v. 17).

Another servant holds up his puny mina and says proudly, "Sir, here is your mina; I have kept it laid away in a piece of cloth. I was afraid of you, because you are a hard man. You take out what you did not put in and reap what you did not sow" (vv. 20–21).

Today, we will study this parable to see if we can gain insight into what it means to put money to work in the kingdom of God.

1. Pray for God's light as you study the Scripture today. Ask him to guide you to understand what you are called to do.

2. Read Luke 19:11–24. The parables of Jesus are stories that make a point. What do you think the point of this parable is?

3. Read Psalm 24:1 and 50:10–12. Who owns the material resources with which we have been entrusted?

4. Why do you think one of the servants laid away the minas he was given in a safe place?

5. How did the servant who held on to his minas view the king?

6. What did the king call the man who held onto the minas rather than investing them?

7. What does God expect us to do with resources we have?

8. As stewards of God's property, we look for ways we can put resources to work to advance God's kingdom, not our own. What investments have you made with which you think God is most pleased?

9. What has been the return on those investments?

10. Like the servants in the parable, God has entrusted us with various gifts and talents. We are responsible, for a period of time, to put them to work, to invest them, to bring a return. Certainly we need to use the resources that come our way to provide food, clothing, and shelter for our families, but decisions about what we spend and how we invest should always be carefully considered in light of how they will bring the greatest return for the kingdom of God, for the owner of all we are and have. Take some time to reflect upon your kingdom investments and how you might more effectively put resources to work. Pray for guidance.

Scripture Memory Verses

Psalm 50:9–10: "I have no need of a bull from your stall or of goats from your pens, for every animal of the forest is mine, and the cattle on a thousand hills."

WEEK 4

Who Is My Neighbor?

GROUP DISCUSSION GUIDE

This week we explored what it means to love our neighbor. Loving God and neighbor is a key part of what it means to follow Jesus. The Good Samaritan responded to the plight of the traveler with compassion and practical assistance. When we love our neighbor, we are investing in God's kingdom.

1. Open your time together in prayer, asking the Holy Spirit to guide your conversation.

2. How do you typically respond to panhandlers?

3. What are the two commandments Jesus taught that were most important?

4. How do these commandments relate to one another?

5. In the parable of the good Samaritan, Jesus chose the example of the good neighbor to be a person from a despised race. Who might this Samaritan represent in our present culture?

6. The Samaritan went near the mugged man and felt compassion for him. Where might you go today to find people who are struggling with difficult circumstances?

7. Can you give examples of times when getting near people in need resulted in growing your feelings of compassion?

8. The priest and the Levite passed by the injured man without getting involved. What are some reasons we might hesitate to get involved with people in need?

9. The Samaritan took the injured man to a place where he could be cared for. What are some of those places in your community?

10. The Samaritan invested in the mugged man's recovery. What are some investments you made to compassion ministries that you feel gave a great return?

11. What does it mean to be led by the Spirit rather than driven by need?

12. Spend time together in prayer asking God to reveal ways you can make a compassionate difference in the lives of the invisible in your community.

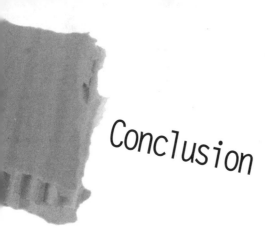

Conclusion

Congratulations! You have successfully completed this in-depth study from God's Word regarding compassion for the poor. When you read Scripture in the context of spending time with the poor, the Word of God comes alive with fresh meaning. Caring for the poor with the compassion of Christ is not peripheral to what it means to be a Christian. Like the Lord said about Josiah, defending the cause of the poor and needy is part of what it means to know God.

My prayer is that you have been challenged to consider what the Bible teaches about compassion for the poor. Once we know what Scripture teaches, we can act upon it with the confidence that we have God's heart. We can trust that God loves us and knows what is best for us. Your life will be enriched as you discover the hidden treasure of spending time with people who may be poor in terms of monetary wealth, but whom God considers rich. May you experience the blessing of being near God as you draw near to the brokenhearted.